# ABOUT THE BOOK

This book (**Freight Brokerage Unleashed**) is to raise leaders, all around the globe and change their mindset to stand up and say to themselves YES I can, YES I can become business owner, YES I can still make it no matter what comes my way. You should always believe in yourself worth, it might take longer than expected but always believe that you can make it by striving harder.

This book is written to encourage you and guard you through on how to land big deal from cold calling, quoting, prospecting, following up, onboarding and landing as client.

# CHAPTER I

# RATE BUY VS SPOT BUY

**SALES IN LOGISTICS BUSINESS**

Like we all know, Logisticians populate almost every field, from retail to finance to government. In the private sector, they handle shipping, distribution, warehousing and quick deliveries to customers. **Logistics** is a relatively narrow field, and **job** growth is on par with the average for all occupations.

Thus, what we do basically as broker in logistics is to provide excellence in transportation and logistics services. Source for new client and also freight from existing clients by doing a spot bid when there's a bid send by client. Most times, some clients send rate buy for freights in this case you have to be extremely careful before you accept the offer.

Spot buy: This is a process of sending rate to client for a particular shipment. In most cases, spot buy allows the salesperson to dictate and control the market rate between the client and carriers. Most salesperson would prefer having client send shipment without rate so they can make good profit margin when clients accept their bid as it make the job more easier to get a carrier to move the freight without losing money.

Rate buy: This is a process whereby client send rate for you to move that particular shipment not considering your options. Brokers benefit from this only when you are a truck owner or you already have a dedicated carrier that would accept a less rate from the rate client sent.

As a sales person there are some things that you have to take into consideration:

I. **Client satisfaction:** Always learn to deliver on every promise you give a customer. Respect clearly all the instructions on the tender given and ensure all details are carefully noted and delivery is met on the date stipulated, noting carefully the equipment, securements and every other stipulation on the tender won.

II. **Prompt Notice:** In the event of any delay or non-coverage of a shipment, be ahead of the game and know far ahead of the pick-up or delivery and do advise the client on this and give them prior notice to forestall any issues.

III. **Noting Information:** Always read through carefully the tender before placing any bids, special attention to weight, equipment, commodity, urgency of pickup, date of delivery before any tender is placed.

**Factors that may affect rates.**
- Holiday Seasons.
- Agricultural Season
- Fuel Price
- Natural hazard/ disaster

As a sales person, you consider the above before placing your bids as this would determine how high or low you bid.
You also consider customer relationship, as there are times you have to reduce your rates as a means of keeping your client happy. All you need to find is your "sweet spot" when you bid i.e. not too high not too low just right.

**Tools to guide you in bidding or getting fair rates.**

**Google Maps:** This is a free tool that helps you to calculate the distance between one city or state as the case may be.

**DAT Rate View:** This is the tool provided by DAT, which helps you to calculate the rate per mile putting into consideration the present fuel rate across a particular lane, this helps well also when it comes to negotiating. This also shows the amount of trucks in the area, which can help you to bid below the amount you normally would as you have an idea about how easy or hard the shipment would be. Other things you would consider; having a database of the load covered previously (lane history) could help you to responds to bidding fast and easy all you need do is to copy and paste the previous rate figures in your present bidding process since is the lane, same weight and commodity

For, a startup company this tools would help a great deal. Saves undue stress and time as it helps you reach a quick decision. But also, intuition as a part to play.

*Quick memory of my first years in Logistical sales. Since the moment the bid came over my email, I wanted to not work with them. I struggled to pick up the massive bid that was on my desk. Even though emails and calls were piling up, I refused to touch the bid against all that were pushing me to see this great opportunity. Something in my gut, my own intuition said STOP! I never did the massive bid and one Friday afternoon as I was leaving the office, I took the massive printed bid on my desk and dumped it in the trash can next to my desk and walked out of my office for the weekend. For a moment, as I was shutting the lights off a voice told me that I was stupid to throw away such an opportunity. Another office within my network, took up the torch and finished the bid. You see…..this bid was for "General Motors" at it was at the fall of 2007. Just 6 months later, GM filed for a massive government bailout and all the carriers hauling their freight was left high and dry with massive invoices unpaid. It is imperative that you don't look at all the glitter and glam of the bid, but that you also follow your intuition. If you ever get a feeling to walk away, you need to trust yourself to just walk away! Sales is also about knowing when to say NO, as much as it is to say YES!

# CHAPTER III

# STAYING OUT OF THE GUTTER

Staying out of the gutters does not mean physical tunnels in our homes, streets or communities, rather STAYING OUT OF GUTTERS here is that unpleasing situations that you've experienced in your life, businesses and or in company as CEO the good news is "What comes around goes around" I would share with you my experience and how I was able to STAY OUT OF THE GUTTERS! Everything I learned in business came from the root of my grandma's nagging! She has always told me, "treat them how you want to be treated, on the first day on the sales floor was not anything extraordinary, on the contrary it was a disaster. Well, all my colleagues were younger and vibrant than me and that meant, I had to work harder to get noticed! How would I get noticed? I would land the biggest deal this company had ever seen and that is exactly what I did, I came in everyday looking for the biggest fish to fry, speaking life and due diligence into my work! Day after day, I was insulted by what I saw in front of me, women going to the bosses office and getting their quotes, as I sat in front of my screen, no matter how I twisted my voice it always came out the same.. Squeaky and terrible! I was so very critical of the words that flew through my head and I wondered, GOD... WHY ME! (GUTTER) Why do I have to do this today, why at this time in my life am I raising 3 girls and pushing myself like this for nothing, while others are rising up the ladder.

Well, one uneventful day, my boss came screaming in my office slewing words of vulgarities about how he is going to FIRE MY A......! (GUTTER) He went on to say how much of a disappointment I am to him and how he had to sit through each meeting as he had to explain my high salary and no performance to upper management. Now.... this was the moment, that I could have jerked back with some mouthy and salty comment, well... I was born African and believe me, I had some SPUNK! My veins in my neck were bulging as I swallowed my pride as this arrogant jerk of a boss was WORD vomiting all over my small and tiny office (GUTTER), that is if you could call it office, for it was no bigger than a 4 x 4 cage! I wondered, would this be the day that I just walk out! I shook my head (GUTTER), well I know I did in my mind. However, in reality, I was looking at my shoes and wondering, will I ever get a new pair? (GUTTER)Then, I remembered my elderly grandma and my 3 beautiful girls and said.. NOPE, today was not the day!

From week to week, I kept making these cold calls to manufacturers asking if I could be one that could handle their freight as a freight broker?! Then one day, I got a call back, it was a very nice and warm phone call and the client on the other end, just made my day. He told me he is going to send me an email and I need to get back to him ASAP if I wanted to get in on the deadline before they made some choices on their freight providers. My hands were shaking as I wrote down the details of what he needed and kept hitting refresh on my email, waiting for that email to come. There it was! The GOLD! The biggest FISH! The GOLDEN TICKET! I was shaking as I printed the email to go get a quote. I then printed and stopped, I carefully took my scissors out of my desk drawer and cut the top of the quote request off, taking off the name. You see..... I saw all those younger and prettier women go into my bosses office, and they never closed the deal... all those quotes & yet only one of them closed the deal. If I was going to be the biggest winner I had to play this cool...........and collectively. I took 2 large breaths and walked confidently as I possibly could muster and asked for 4 quotes. My boss half smiled and looked at me and said, "it is about time" His sarcasm never even made me flinch, because I knew that these 4 quotes were my golden ticket! I was going to be the best!

As I typed the quotes back to the client, I never flinched, I just sent and believed! As days went by, I followed up on the 3rd day and to my words "GOLDEN TICKET".. I got the ticket to the fast track! These 4 quotes landed me 6 million in sales my first 90 days and a drop trailer contract that paid $500 per day into Mexico! As I went into my bosses office that day, his jaw dropped and then he sat me down and said, "My dear (ha! Now I am DEAR???).. You know you haven't been a strong leader and upper management doesn't trust you, you came to work for us highly recommended and this is your 1st sale in 4 months you have been here. I sat back and listened as I could see his bulging eyes lying to me. He said, "let me take credit for this one because you know you are unreliable"... You see that day, I backed down, let him take credit! Over the course of the next year, I had many other BIG FISH and BIGGER GOLDEN TICKETS! Sometimes, you just have to take it for the team. Years, later, I own my own brokerage firm and never once did I ever take any of those clients without consulting! On the contrary, I waited 5 years before I went to previous employer and said, "I will be pursuing 2 of these clients... " He laughed and said, "I was wondering about you"....You see... always and always, no matter if you feel offended or looked over.. Always! "Remember...treat them the way you want to be treated" Now the question is, I could have decided to remain in "GUTTER" by using the above experience as an excuses to quit the job but I didn't rather I choose to fight it by keeping calm just to STAY OUT OF THE GUTTER, no business or job is easy to run but if you must SUCCEED out of the GUTTER then you have to be patient, have perseverance, be humble and hardworking, this are the 4 keys to STAYING OUT OF THE GUTTERS.

## CHAPTER III

## COLD CALL

Cold call is defined as the solicitation of business from

potential customers who have had no prior contact with the salesperson conducting the call. Cold call is an attempt to convince potential customers to purchase either the salesperson's product or service. Salesperson in Brokerage company like ours make cold calls to old and potential customers for trucks and shipments

## Cold Call Tips:

Cold calling potential prospects can be frustrating and hard, whether you are doing it in person or on the phone, it is your job to warm up a potential customer.
(a) plan all your questions in advance
(b) Don't follow any cold script
(c) Don't attempt to sell on your first cold call
(d) Don't overwhelm your prospect during first meeting
(e) Find out what benefit will make your prospect buy from you.

## How to win back old customers

Lost customers represent a huge area of opportunity. Former customers understand your product or services and how you operate, they often left for a reason that is easily corrected.

## Why do customers leave?

If you know why customers leave, it's much easier to win them back. Here are the top reasons why customers may stop doing business with you.

1. They were wooed away by a competitor promising better prices, better service or other benefits
2. The organization has changed, and new management is not aware of the strengths of your services or products because the information was not passed on to them by their predecessors
3. You or your company failed to deliver as promised
4. You or your company let trust or respect erode in the relationship.

A recent of survey of former customers by Fortune 1000 company showed that about a third said they would return to the company they dropped if approached.

**Three steps to win back program**
1. Find out why customer stopped buying, search records for clues and then call the customer and ask what went wrong. Try to put together a special offer that addresses why you lost the account in the first place.

2. Research the customer's present situation. The customer business may have changed. If you understand what happened, you can create a better offer that will take advantage of those changes
3. Make the contact, call the former customer and let him or her know that you want to get their business back.

**Importance of following up:**
1. No salesman ever has made the sale 100% of the time. The average close rate in sales is around 6%
2. It takes 5 steps to achieve 80% targeted goal.
i. 2% of sales are made on the 1st contact
ii. 3% of sales are made on the 2nd contact
Iii. 5% of sales are made on the 3rd contact
iv. 10%of sales are made on the 4th contact
v. 80% of sales are made on the 5th-12th contact.

**Sales statistics**
i. 48% of people never follow up with a prospect
ii. 25% of sales people make a second contact and stop
iii 12% of sales people only make three contact and stop
iv. Only 10% of sales people make more than three contacts
v. 2% of sales are made on the first contact
vi. 3% of sales are made on the second contact
vii. 5% of sales are made on the third contact
viii. 10% of sales made on the fourth contact
ix. 80% of sales are made on the fifth to twelfth contact

**When to make contact**

Always make at least 6 call attempts!, Your chances of making contact increase to 90%

**Best day of the week:**
1. Thursday
2. Wednesday
3. Friday
4. Monday
5. Tuesday

**Best times of the day:**
1. 4pm-5pm
2. 5pm-6pm
3. 8am-9am
4. 9am-10am
5. 3pm-4pm

There is a 49% difference between Thursday and Tuesday. There is a 164% better Rate at 4pm than 1pm.

    *I learned the hard way that busyness is a silent killer. The truth is you have to make time for cold calls and balance the current client you have. I have learned that when you are starting out you will wear so many hats the best thing to do is at the chance you get is to hire a part time staff to do all your administrative duties that are eating your time and focus on this portion of the business. You must be always COLD CALLING in logistics. There shouldn't be a day that goes by that you are not putting in your 10 - 15 new cold calls.

    Over a decade ago, I had a client that he would just know my voice after so many months of calling him. Well, those months turned to years and the years kept going by. Yet, without fail, I had my alarm go off on my cell phone that was programmed into my calendar that I would call him on the 3rd Thursday of the month at exactly 3 pm. He knew when I would call him and he got used to that consistency and familiarity. There was even times, that I would laugh and joke that he would be missing my voice as the Thanksgiving Holiday would be coming up, "should I call you on Wednesday", I laughed. You see, we had nothing much in common except this date on the calendar! For purposes of discussion, I will call him EARL and that one client landed me only one shipment, that one shipment grossed me over 5 K. It was worth all the calls over the years, a total of 59 calls. So that means my payout was $83.00 per call or $83.00 for 3 minutes of my time! Everything that is measured is managed and measuring & managed = profit!

## CHAPTER IV
## 8 SALES STEPS

Before it ends this is how it begins, determination, focus and trusting your sales teams by sharing your vision, idea with each and every one of them, it would go beyond knowing how to close a sales deal with a customer and the sales steps you and your sales teams follows when connecting a customer or client to the sales channel. This must be done before you start making contact with the prospect customer and it continue long after the sales is finalized.

Understanding sales steps encompasses all major customer interactions from prospecting to selling and to nurturing stage.

**Benefit Of Sales Steps**

⇨ It gives you better understand every stage of your sales pipeline
⇨ It develop more effective sales and marketing strategies
⇨ It moves prospects along the buying process more quickly
⇨ It smoothly onboard new hires when expanding your sales team as well having a well-thought-out sales steps allows you to create and nurture long-lasting customer relationships – which can transform into higher customer lifetime value, reducing customer acquisition cost, more customer referrals, and increased profit potential.

Creating a Sales Steps that Works for Your Team
Before you can develop a well-defined sales process, you need to understand your sales team's existing steps or lacks. Once you know what you're working with, you can decide which steps to take as it progresses

Double check your sales team activities to identify their strengths, weaknesses, or gaps in their steps. Is there any point at which prospect interest tends to drop? Are your teams following up multiple times? How long does it take to close a sale from first point of contact to signing the deal?
Chat with your sales team a one-on-one conversation with each of your sales teams for feedback, you would have a lot about current sales practices and how they go about turning prospects into customers.

If you aren't sure how to guide the conversation, pick a recent customer acquisition to discuss and ask these questions:

How was the lead first contacted? Email, phone, social media, or in person ?
How many tries did it take to get a response from the lead?

How frequently did you reach out?
What questions did you ask during your first conversation?
How did you qualify the lead into trigger statement?
How did you demo the solution? Video call, phone, in-person presentation?
What were the biggest sales objections voiced by the prospect?
What was the timeline between initial contact and signing the deal?
Did you follow up with the customer after the sale?
Visualize the process you want to create. Based on existing customer data and the firsthand information gathered from your sales teams, breakdown the buyer's process into clearly-defined sales steps. Use a recent customer acquisition for reference and map out each step of the process. Determine what action prospects must take to move on to the next stage, so

### The 8 Sales Steps
Even though your sales process should be tailored to your specific teams and solution, these are general steps we recommend including in your sales process. Depending on what you discover about your sales team with the framework above, your process might be shorter or include some variation of these steps.

### Step 0: Prospecting "Ground ZERO"
Before you can sell anything, you need someone to sell to. That's why you should start with lead generation, also known as prospecting.

This step involves creating a list of potential leads and conducting preliminary research to find out their contact information. Sales teams often leverage social media, their existing network, and customer referrals to find qualified leads. You can use a free tool like Hunter to verify the accuracy of your list.

If you already have a solid customer base, spend some time creating an ideal customer profile. This will allow you to identify your audience segments and help your sales team target each of them more effectively. After all, different types of outreach work better for different types of prospects.

### Step 1: Connecting

Every cold email or phone call is the start of a new relationship with a potential client. This step is your only chance to make a good first impression, which is critical if you want the chance to demonstrate the benefits of your product or service.

So, how can you make sure you're making a great impression? Be as relevant and personable as possible. Use your background knowledge of the company and lead to build rapport.

Remember, the goal here is to get the lead to see you as someone who can provide value – not just as a salesperson trying to make quota. If you'd like more detailed advice on doing effective cold outreach, check out our comprehensive guide to running a cold email campaign.

### Step 2: Qualifying

During your initial phone call or early in your email conversation, it's important to ask qualifying questions. After all, you want to make sure you're pitching to the right person (that is, are you in direct contact with the decision-maker?), ask about their needs, and assess their pain points.

Ask questions that help you determine how they will benefit from your product or service. Are they an ideal customer? Are they ready to make a purchase ASAP – or do they need to wait for the new budget to get approved?

There are plenty of frameworks available to help you understand whether or not a lead is likely to buy. For example, the BANT framework looks at a prospect's budget, authority to make a decision, need for your solution, and timing.

Your aim is to see if there's a mutual fit. Once a prospect has been qualified, then go back and do more research about their company so you can tailor your pitch.

### Step 3: Demonstrating Value

Setting up a product demo gives you the chance to show off your solution. Whether it's an in-person meeting or you're using a video conferencing platform, research and preparation is key to delivering a winning product demo.

The more you can personalize the demo to fit the prospect's immediate needs, the better you'll be able to sell them on the benefits. Frame the product as a solution to a problem facing the prospect or their business – and help them understand what they'll miss out on if they don't buy.

### Step 4: Addressing Objections

Even after you deliver a killer sales pitch, your prospect will likely have a few things they need cleared up before committing to a purchase. But that's not a bad thing! Listening to your prospect's sales objections gives you an opportunity to understand their perspective and reframe your sales pitch accordingly.

At this step of the sales process, you should try to identify and address any concerns that arise after the demo. Reiterate the cost of not purchasing your product (i.e. leverage the fear of missing out on a good deal) and answer whatever questions the prospect has about your solution, brand, and prices.

If you need specific tips on addressing common sales objections, we've written about that, too.

### Step 5: Closing the Deal

Now that you've addressed the prospect's main concerns, the finish line is in sight! You're almost ready to ask them to sign on the dotted line.

But first, you must create a proposal, negotiate the details, and get buy-in from decision-makers on both sides. Only then can you move on to signing the deal and officially landing your newest customer.

### Step 6: Onboarding

The sales team's role doesn't end after closing the deal. Depending on the size of your company, it's often beneficial if the same sales teams who landed the deal continues to work with the customer during onboarding. This creates a sense of continuity and builds on their already-developed relationship.

Onboarding can include delivering the product, getting the client set up with your solution, and providing any necessary support. Not only should your sales team help set new customers up for success during onboarding, but it's also time to start thinking about customer retention. Shift your focus to finding out what it will take to keep your customer happy and for them to stay on as a long-term client.

### Step 7: Following Up

The final (and often-overlooked) stage is following up. One of the biggest mistakes salespeople make is not following up enough. This is true not only in closing sales (the average deal takes five follow-ups to close!), but also in nurturing a long-term customer relationship and repeat buyer.

Nurturing a new customer involves supporting them after the sale, answering questions, and keeping them happy with their purchase. Stay in contact, maintain open lines of communication, and look for opportunities to up sell or cross-sell certain solutions.

After the product is delivered or the customer has been using it for a while, follow-up to find out if they are still satisfied with their experience. This is also the perfect opportunity to ask for referrals.

Never Stop Looking for Ways to Improve Your Sales Process
After you've interacted with your sales teams, reviewed your sales history, and created your first sales process, track any changes to your sales activities and metrics. How does the new process affect your sales pipeline, revenue, and customer satisfaction?

As your sales team and business evolve, go back and revisit the logic behind your sales process to see if it still makes sense. Check in with your teams periodically and monitor their sales activities to see how well the current process is working – and don't get discouraged if you constantly find new ways to tweak it.

To some extent, your sales process will always be a work in progress – but the payoff of having an efficient, effective process will make it worthwhile.

**Step 8. Managing Customers Expectations**
Knowing and understanding customer expectations at the outset, helps your company to work with the customer to set the expectations at an optimum level. Don't set the expectations too high lest you fail. Setting them too low can leave your customer feeling that your company is incompetent.
*"We are in the customer service business. Our goal must be to exceed our customers' expectations everyday". –* **Dave Thomas**
True customer satisfaction and stellar customer service can only happen through a complete and proper understanding of the customer expectations. Unless your company knows what they want, who they are and what they expect, it would be difficult to even match up to the expectations. Companies should make it a practice to ask their customers whether they have been able to meet or exceed their expectations through the products or services and customer service. It is only based on this feedback that companies can assuredly know that they match customer expectations. The reality now is that customer expectations are continually on the rise, and unless companies are attuned to them,

they will fall short of those expectations leading to customer ire and attrition.

However companies approach this, there is no escaping that it is customer expectations that sets and raises the bar for customer service and the resultant satisfaction or dissatisfaction. This obviously affects customer loyalty and if they are displeased it is unlikely that they will return. Pleased customers will return but delighted customers will speak positively of your company through every possible channel. This happens when your company has consistently exceeded customer expectations. Customer testimonials are great free publicity that eliminates the first thread of doubt that most prospective customers have. So what are some of unchanging and universal facts of customer expectations?

– Even before entering into a business relationship, customers have a perceived notion of what they would like to receive from the relationship. Most often the customer expectations encompass receiving more than what they expect and pay for.

– Customers expect that companies will be dependable, honest, swift and courteous. Companies can exceed these expectations by ensuring that each experience a customer has leaves them feeling happy and knowing that they have commitment from the company

– Customer expectations operate from two levels. One level is where they expect a certain kind of service and product and when they receive it they are satisfied. The other level, which is the most desired one, is the one where they expect to get more than what they are receiving.

– Among the top in customer expectations is relationship building. Customers expect a personalized relationship with the company they are doing business with and are happy when it is on-going and consistent. They also prefer if the company connects with them to strike and deal and when it is done, they expect to interact with the same person each time they connect with the company so that they do not have repeat any information. This creates a bond and a feeling of oneness, which is very healthy for the association.

– Customer expectations also include that companies will keep their promise on everything committed. It is always better to under-promise and over-deliver keeping in mind the competitive marketplace that everyone is operating in. Broken promises can have serious impacts on customer expectations and leave them feeling highly irritated with a possibility of severing the relationship. It is essential and difficult but not impossible to manage customer satisfaction and one of the metrics of doing so is managing customer expectations. To prevent souring of customer relationships, companies must carefully set and meet customer expectations. If it seems like something is going out of hand, it may be time to re-set or re-establish those expectations in order to manage them better.

As we said earlier on, customer expectations set the bar for customer satisfaction. It would benefit companies immensely to understand customer expectations from this aspect:

– Companies can know for sure which level of customer service keeps customers satisfied and what takes that satisfaction to a level of delight and wow

– Customer expectations when properly understood can be disseminated to employees as knowledge, making it easier for them to service customers according to those standards

– Once meeting customer expectations becomes a standard, it paves the way to exceed these expectations and make customers become enthusiastic advocates of your company and its service.

– Having a grasp of customer expectations also lowers the number of complaints. Also in the event of a complaint, resolution become quicker and more effective since you would know what the customer expects as an outcome

All customers are different and so are their needs. Their understanding of stellar customer service is also different and to know what the customer feels, it is imperative that companies ask them rather than going by what they believe they 'know'.

Sometimes companies may find that the customer expectations are beyond what they can deliver – for example a company may not have the infrastructure to support a 24×7 online chat service. They would need to work around that to be able to provide what the customer needs. Also products and services must be priced according to what the customer finds suitable and yet remain profitable for your company. That is why knowing customer expectations at the outset is crucial – it allows you to understand them better and weave them in to your company's policies and customer service strategy.

Knowing and understanding customer expectations at the outset, helps your company to work with the customer to set the expectations at an optimum level. Don't set the expectations too high lest you fail. Setting them too low can leave your customer feeling that your company is incompetent. Let your customers know what level of service they can expect, the kind of support you provide and the established standards in your company to ensure that their needs are fulfilled. Every company would have a different method of satisfying the customer expectations just as every customer would have a different set of needs and expectations. What would work well is if companies were to treat every customer as the first, the only and the one person who could give them the finest testimonial. This will drive everyone in the company to serve the customer with the highest level of service and provide the best products possible.

Before companies can strive to exceed customer expectations, they must first reach a level where they consistently meet those expectations. It is only then that you would have a set of satisfied customers. Building on these levels of satisfaction, companies can aim to exceed them thereby creating experiences that wow and delight customers. These are the experiences that the customers would excitedly share with others, giving a boost to your company's reputation and earning for it more customers.

Having said that companies must strive to exceed expectations, there will be times when companies will fail to please. Customers will be dissatisfied and the reasons could be many. Untrained staff, technology failure, human error, heightened expectations due to past great service levels – are some of the reasons for a service lapse leaving customers unhappy. The good news is that these occasional lapses are tolerated by customers since your company was consistent in providing great service. All they would expect is that the right is wronged swiftly and there is a genuine effort to make it better and ensure that the error is not repeated. Customers know what good service is, what they can expect and what companies can give. These form the customer expectations and companies that get a grip on these expectations are the ones who can not only meet them but also consistently exceed them.

## How to manage customer expectations

Meeting expectations rather than exceeding them isn't an excuse to stop trying to satisfy your customers. It's just a smarter way of managing these expectations in a way that's good for your customers and your business.

You can't meet everyone's expectations, so you'll have to be selective about your battlefields. Here are our tried and true principles that we've collected to help you manage your customer expectations.

**7 Principles for Managing Customer Expectations** :- *Michelle (Digital Customer Service)*

*If you've ever visited a major fast food chain, then you might know what it's like to have your expectations crash and burn.*

The way they present their hamburgers – juicy patties topped with melted cheese, crisp lettuce and fresh tomatoes – could get just about anyone yearning for a bite. So you order yourself one at the counter and receive a neatly wrapped package.

And then you unwrap it.

What you actually get is a mediocre sandwich at best. The patties are pressed dry, the cheese looks more like rubber than something edible, the lettuce is wilted and you have to take off the top bun just to find the teeny tiny tomato.

The challenge with customer expectations is rooted in a dilemma. To *win* customers, you need to promise value ; to *keep* customers, you need to manage the expectations created by that promise.

**1. Define and adhere to baseline expectations**

There are some things that every business needs to adhere to, which are "baseline expectations." These are mostly set by industry standards and even by laws or regulations. No matter how low-cost an airline is is, for example, losing a customer's luggage is unacceptable. If you run a restaurant, it's legally required to follow food safety guidelines.

Every online shop needs a secured payment system and a minimum set of contact options for support. For online businesses located in Germany, an imprint page is a legal requirement.

Technical aspects like a minimum loading speed are also considered a baseline requirement since its estimated up to 53% of visitors will leave if it takes longer than 3 seconds to load the page.

**2 Create a strategic position to excel in**

After making sure you're meeting the baseline expectations, strategically positioning your business will help to narrow the focus. To define those areas you want to excel in and raise your customers' expectations.

This means deliberately picking areas for over performance *and* for underperformance. Amazon, for example, underperforms in web design. Their website isn't exactly polished. They've never bothered to follow design trends. But they over perform in usability and selection. Their website loads quickly and customers can find practically everything for an affordable price.

Asking yourself questions like, *"Who am I targeting?"* and *"What do they care about?"* will help you get closer to defining a strategic position for your business.

To define "who," you can use a method like customer personas . When it comes down to choosing which strategy you'd like to adopt, you could use a framework like Porter's Generic Strategies . It analyzes how businesses can situate themselves against their competitors. The three strategies are:

- **Cost leadership strategy:** Focuses on offering low prices (e.g. Walmart).

- **Differentiation strategy:** Focuses on a unique feature that sets your product/service apart from competitors (e.g. Apple).

- **Focus strategy:** Focus on niche markets (in combination with cost leadership or differentiation) (e.g. Porsche).

These strategies can be generally applied to almost every area of business, product or service. Once you've defined your strategy, it's then carried out through your business design, marketing and communication strategy, along with tracking and monitoring techniques.

### 3 Design your business accordingly

Whichever strategy you've chosen, you'll need to deliver. Your business needs to be structured in a way that will help you achieve this.

Amazon's strategy is targeting high-choice with low-cost, with a focus on offering fast delivery. In order to meet these expectations, Amazon needs to have a huge reach, a top notch logistics system, and a strong bargaining position over its suppliers.

Many technical companies set their expectations for their customers in a pleasant user experience. To make sure their business design supports this, they may implement a tool like Userlane that helps guide a user through onboarding and increase engagement.

### 4 Communicate accordingly

The next step in carrying out your business strategy is sending the right messages to your customers. This is all about making sure that your customers perceive you how you want to be perceived.

*When your website says you offer 24/7 customer support for your users, don't make this hollow words: make sure you can live up to that promise.*

How you market and communicate your business's strong points will influence how your customers set their expectations of you. By emphasizing where you overachieve, you're guiding your customers' expectations to those areas. And since your business design has been set up to help you excel in your strategic areas, you'll be able to successfully meet those expectations.

Seeing that Amazon's strong points lie in selection and fast delivery, you can be sure that this is where they choose to create their advertisement campaigns, like in this commercial for their Prime service.

They've guided the expectations of their audience through their communication, and then they've made sure to manage them. Anyone who's ordered through Prime knows that they will pull through.

The next time you're thinking of how to communicate and market your business, consider that what you're showing them has a great deal of influence on their expectations. When you communicate honestly, you won't let your customers down (I'm looking at you, fast food restaurants).

**5 Monitor and highlight the right metrics**

The areas that you choose to compete on should define your most important metrics . Whether it be fast delivery or providing top-notch customer support, you can track and monitor these areas to gauge how you're doing.

Say, like Amazon, one of your focuses is fast delivery. You could track delivery speed, or the number of late deliveries. When you have concrete numbers to go from, you can tell more objectively how effectively your business design is supporting your strategies or if it needs some readjusting.

A tool like Geckoboard can help you track these metrics and display them to your team members. By making these numbers known team-wide, everyone will have a better idea of what's going on and what areas to focus on.

**6 Favor transparency**

Transparency isn't just a pillar of good communication . Being transparent with your customers can be a meaningful way to manage expectations that doesn't actually take a lot of effort.

Keeping your customers informed on what's going on can save you a lot of headache when it comes to readjusting expectations– which is inevitable to happen. Instead of waiting for disappointment to arise when plans change, let your customers know.

*What I learned from interacting with customers in real time is to be honest with them. Transparency is key. They might ask a question and I don't know the answer. They are more patient and understanding if I tell them what I'm doing - checking their account, escalating the question - and most importantly, telling them how long I think it'll take to get it fixed.*

If you're a business that makes deliveries to customers, using a tool like ParcelPerform is beneficial because it can send your customers automatic notifications to know when they should expect to receive their packages and notify them of any changes or delays.

**7 Aim for consistency**

One of the reasons a business like Starbucks is so successful is because you always know what to expect, no matter where in the world you are.

Consistency is a process that shows itself over time and requires ongoing attention. It can easily be overlooked, though, so formalizing processes within the business can help make sure that you're staying on track.

These include training, standardizing processes, and creating and following checklists .

Once you've begun working on a consistent level, managing customer expectations will become even easier because customers who've interacted with you before will know what to expect from you. Not only that, but you'll also be able to meet them since it's become a normal routine.

**Met? Managed.**

Managing customer expectations results in positive returns for both businesses and customers alike. Businesses are able to meet the needs of their customers and customers take away a pleasant experience.

It's no impossible feat to manage your customers' expectations. All it takes is some time, mindful behavior and practice. This will transform for the better the way you perceive your audience and interactions with them.

# CHAPTER V

# TIME AND CONSISTENCY

**Time**
Is something we deal with every day, and something that everyone thinks they understand. However, **time** is the indefinite continued progress of existence and events in the past, present and future regarded as a whole.
Another way of looking at time is as the totality of three separate elements: the past, the present and the future.

**Past**
May be defined as those events which occurred before a given point in time, events which are usually considered to be fixed and immutable. It can be accessed through memory or, since the advent of written language, recorded history. The study of the past, in particular as it relates to humans, is called history.

**Present**
May be defined as the time associated with the events perceived directly and for the first time, i.e. not as a recollection of the past or as a speculation of the future. It is equivalent to the word "now", and is the period of time located between the past and the future. Just how long a period of time the present incorporates, however, depends on the context, and can vary from an infinitesimal or duration less moment to a day to a whole era, depending on how it is being used.

**Future**
Is the indefinite time period after the present moment. It is the portion of the projected timeline that is anticipated to occur, and may be considered as potentially infinite in its extent, or as circumscribed and finite, depending on the context. While some people may see the future as fixed and predetermined, most see it as essentially unknown (and perhaps unknowable), and open to many different possibilities and permutations.

**CONSISTENCY**
The love of a father has its essence in on-going care, compassion, kindness, help, teaching, guiding and friendship. Love demonstrated by a father sees no restriction of time; there is never any inconvenience; there is never any inconsistency; there is never a withholding; and there is never an end. A father's love is timeless extending to the point of one's departure from this world. It is a love manifested in words and actions that leaves a legacy to a child to pass on to their own family unit as well as to those around them. It is a love so strong that its' glow and manifestation is not limited by distance nor by time. Consistency makes the rain drops to create holes in the rock. Whatever is difficult can be done easily with regular attendance, attention and action.

The key to success is Time and Consistency. And right now, the only way for you to actually take action is to believe in yourself.

And, don't expect immediate recognition after you have made positive changes. There has to be consistency in your behavior and performance over time. Don't think that by reading a book, and changing some of your behaviors, that tomorrow will bring you recognition, or a promotion. Often people get discouraged or disillusioned by expecting everyone to instantly see the positive changes they have made. Allow time to work to your advantage

If your desire is pale and flabby, your achievements will also take on that hue and consistency

Consistency is the fruit of the tree of success. The more you do something effectively and with a goal in mind, the better you will get at it and the more you will feel fulfilled.

The Bible also tells one story with consistency. It was written over a 1,500-year time span, on three continents, and by 40 authors people from every walk of life, like kings, shepherds, fishermen, and tax collectors. Yet the Bible tells one story from beginning to end: God's love and salvation for man and how he came into this world through Jesus Christ. It's an amazing example of the power of God to write that story for our lives.

Consistency is one of the biggest factors in leading to accomplishment and success.

All winning teams are goal-oriented. Teams like these win consistently because everyone connected with them concentrates on specific objectives. They go about their business with blinders on; nothing will distract them from achieving their aims.

Consistency is a key element, without which a leader is incapable of getting respect, success or even developing confidence in others. In this line of business you need TIME AND CONSISTENCY to excel, clients are not built in a day but it takes time and consistency to win their heart over to your side because there are 1001 brokers out there soliciting for clients like you're doing while some are already signed off with another brokers so it going to take them time to consider your proposals that is if you would continually calling and reminding them.

**CHAPTER VI**

# WINNING THE GAME.

Hungry for a different kind of winning if you must succeed in this game, effective "self-coaching" is the first step to success in your personal and professional relationships. -Action Steps—decide what you want and how you're going to get it. In this kind of game you must set out winning strategies for effective communication, better organization, and time management.

**RULES FOR HOW TO WIN THIS TYPE OF GAME**

**1) SET CLEAR AND EMPOWERING GOALS**

Winning this type of game you must set clear and empowering goals. Goals are of course important for a couple of reasons. Firstly, they help improve your mental focus. When you set goals you work with more urgency and purpose. In other words, they help provide you with a sense of direction for your life and company. As a result your mental focus is driven by the priorities you set that helps you achieve those goals. Secondly, goals enhance your level of commitment and inspire passion. However, in order to fully commit yourself to this journey, you must clearly outline why you want to achieve these goals in the first place.

**2) CONSISTENTLY STRETCH YOUR COMFORT ZONE**

Winning the game you consistently stretch your comfort zone. This is of course important when it comes to goal achievement. After all, everything you want essentially lies outside the boundaries of your comfort zone. You will actually need to step outside your comfort zone to grab a hold of these goals. Unfortunately, a great many people simply don't take this necessary step. They don't take it because every goal comes riddled with problems that must first be overcome. However, little do they realize that overcoming these problems will stretch their comfort zone and move them closer to their prize.

## 3) GENERATE PLENTY OF BAD IDEAS

Winning the game you must generate plenty of bad ideas. As you stretch your comfort zone you will deal with a vast array of problems. Overcoming these problems may not be easy, and many times you might even be forced to think quickly on your feet. As a result you will make some poor choices that won't seem to work in your favor. But that shouldn't stop you from trying again, and again. Life is a number's game. Don't be afraid to repeatedly take a chance on yourself. The more times you try and fail, the higher the likelihood you will succeed the next time around.

## 4) MAKE MISTAKES AND LEARN FROM THEM

Winning the game you must make mistakes and to learn from them. As you repeatedly try new things to overcome your problems, you are bound to make mistakes. Mistakes are simply a part of life, and a part of living that life. They are a natural part of the human experience, and we all of course make mistakes. However, those who don't win at the game of life simply don't take the time to learn from their mistakes. Life only rewards those who learn from the errors of their ways. It rewards those who treat every experience as a lesson that helps them move forward in a better way.

## 5) WORK SMARTER AND HARDER THAN YESTERDAY

Winning the game you must strive to work smarter and harder than yesterday. Those who make progress in life and business do so because they are constantly learning, growing and improving. They are building ever greater momentum toward their goals because they learn, adapt and upgrade their effort, skills, knowledge and methods. They clearly understand that in order to do better they must get better, think faster, and work smarter than the day before. They strive to make consistent improvements in a multitude of ways. Life is after all a game of inches. You gain an edge by beating your best-self today.

## 6) EXPOSE YOURSELF TO NEW IDEAS, PEOPLE AND PLACES

Winning the game you must expose yourself to new ideas, people and places. We only grow and develop ourselves when we experience new things, when we learn something unique, and when we step outside the boundaries of our comfort zone. Expanding your horizons in this way provides you with new perspectives and opportunities for further growth and development. And as you grow, you gain ever deeper insights and understandings into your life and circumstances. You then grow wiser with the passage of time and subsequently make more optimal choices and decisions moving forward.

# CONCLUSION

Rules involved to help you in winning the game aren't complicated, and they're certainly not one of life's great big secrets. We all know and understand these rules, but how many of us actually put these rules into practice?

A great many people don't become high achievers because they are just not willing to put in the work to play the game of life as it was supposed to be played.

Yes, of course life isn't all about rewards and accomplishments. But these rules are not just about that either. These rules are about challenging yourself to live your life to the fullest in the most optimal way possible, so that in the end, there are no regrets.

www.ingramcontent.com/pod-product-compliance
Lightning Source LLC
Chambersburg PA
CBHW031515210526
45464CB00007B/2922